THE YOUNGER BROTHERS

Carl R. Green

❖ and ❖

William R. Sanford

ENSLOW PUBLISHERS, INC.

44 Fadem Road   P.O. Box 38

Box 699   Aldershot

Springfield, N.J. 07081   Hants GU12 6BP

U.S.A.   U.K.

Library of Congress Cataloging-in-Publication Data

Green, Carl R.
    The Younger brothers / Carl R. Green and William R. Sanford.
       p. cm — (Outlaws and lawmen of the Wild West)
    Includes bibliographical references and index.
    ISBN 0-89490-592-9
    1. West (U.S.)—History—1860–1890—Biography—Juvenile
literature. 2. Younger, Cole, 1844–1916—Juvenile literature. 3. Younger,
James, 1848–1902—Juvenile literature. 4. Younger family—Juvenile
literature. 5. Outlaws—West (U.S.)—Biography—Juvenile literature.
[1. Younger, Cole, 1844–1916. 2. Younger, James, 1848–1902. 3. Robbers
and outlaws. 4. West (U.S.)—History—1860–1890.] I. Sanford,
William R. (William Reynolds), 1927– . II. Title. III. Series: Green,
Carl R. Outlaws and lawmen of the Wild West.
F594.G763 1995
978′.02′0922—dc20
[B]   94-30109
                                                  CIP
                                                  AC

Printed in the United States of America

10 9 8 7 6 5 4 3 2 1

Illustration Credits: Carl R. Green and William R. Sanford, p. 11; Library
of Congress, p. 6; National Archives, p. 27; Western History Collections,
University of Oklahoma Library, pp. 7, 15, 20, 21, 29, 30, 33, 37, 38, 40, 41.

Cover Illustration: Michael David Biegel

CONTENTS

AUTHORS' NOTE

This book tells the true story of the four outlaw Younger brothers. In partnership with Frank and Jesse James, the Youngers robbed banks and trains in the lawless years that followed the Civil War. During their lifetimes, their exploits were described in newspapers, magazines, and dime novels. In more recent years, the Youngers have been featured in films and on television. Some of the stories told about them have been made up, but others are true. To the best of the authors' knowledge, all of the events described in this book really happened.

1

THE LIBERTY BANK ROBBERY

When the Civil War ended in 1865, Missouri was still torn by old hatreds. For young Southerners the bitter taste of defeat lingered long after the shooting stopped. Two of the former rebels who carried grudges against the Union were Cole Younger and Jesse James. Jesse had been shot while trying to surrender. As his wound healed, he plotted revenge. The war had taught him to take what he wanted. Robbing a bank filled with Northern dollars seemed like a good way to get even.

Jesse's wound had left him too weak to carry out the robbery. He sent his older brother, Frank, to recruit former members of Quantrill's raiders. Men who had ridden with William Quantrill and his hit-and-run band, he guessed, would know how to rob a bank. One of the old friends Frank looked up was Cole Younger. Cole agreed to the plan. He felt he had little to lose. His

As their fame spread, the James-Younger gang liked to pose for the camera. Standing are Cole Younger (left) and his brother Bob (right). Jesse James (left) and his brother Frank (right) are seated, rifles at the ready.

wartime service with Quantrill had made him a wanted man.[1]

A dozen armed men rode into Liberty, Missouri, on February 13, 1866. The sleepy town hardly stirred. The horsemen pulled up in front of the Clay County Savings Bank. Ten stood guard, while two dismounted and entered the bank. Cashier Greenup Bird saw that they wore the blue coats of Union soldiers. Historians think he was looking at Cole Younger and Frank James.[2]

One of the men told Greenup that he wanted to change a bill. As William Bird, Greenup's son, walked forward to help him, the "customer" drew a gun. An instant later both robbers had jumped the counter. As Greenup later wrote, "[They] demanded all the money in the bank and they wanted it quick."[3]

One bandit struck William with his pistol and pushed him into the vault. William scooped gold and silver coins into the wheat sack he was handed. Outside the vault, the second gunman grabbed bundles of greenbacks and bonds. The sack was soon bulging with

Jesse James, shown here at age seventeen, planned the nation's first daylight bank robbery. To fill out his gang, he turned to old friends from his days with Quantrill's raiders. One of his recruits was the tough, hard-riding Cole Younger.

almost $60,000 in cash, bonds, and coins. Satisfied, the men forced Greenup to join William in the vault. Moments later they ran out to the street and climbed into their saddles.

The Birds pushed at the door of the vault. To their surprise the lock had not latched. They ran to a window, yelling that the bank had been robbed. College students George Wymore and Henry Haynes heard their cries. As the students turned toward the bank, a gang member ordered them to not move. Then, as Haynes took cover, the outlaw opened fired. Wymore was caught in the open. A slug knocked him down and killed him. Firing wildly, the outlaws spurred their horses and rode out of town. Within the hour a heavy snowstorm covered their tracks.

The gang found shelter on the far side of the Missouri River. There they split the loot. Most preferred the silver coins and greenbacks, which could be spent anywhere. Cole and Frank took their share in gold coins and bonds. Cole knew a man in Texas who would pay cash for the gold. In the months to come he cashed the bonds in eastern cities a few at a time.

The Liberty bank holdup was the nation's first peacetime bank robbery. Cole never did admit to his part in it. "I never knew where the bonds came from as I never asked it of the friends who had given them to me to cash," he said.[4] Like his three outlaw brothers, Cole Younger was nobody's fool.

2
THE YOUNGERS HELP POPULATE MISSOURI

Western outlaws often grew up in poor families. That was not true of the Younger brothers. Their dad, Henry Younger, traced his descent back to Valley Forge. His grandfather served there with George Washington. As the nation grew the Youngers did their best to populate it. Henry's father, Charles Lee Younger, was one of seventeen children.

Charles moved to Kentucky in 1807. He had a knack for raising fine horses. Drawn westward, he struck it rich selling mules to Colorado miners. The profits paid for a large farm in Cass County, Missouri. He soon became one of the richest men in the state. In all, Charles fathered nineteen children. Eleven of them were born to women other than his wife.

A streak of outlaw blood seemed to run in the family. Bob, Grat, and Emmett Dalton were Charles's grandsons. Charles's daughter-in-law, Augusta Inskeep, was the aunt of gunman Johnny Ringo. Benjamin Simms, another Inskeep, married Zerelda James. Ben never could control his stepsons, Jesse and Frank James. The stormy marriage ended when he died in a fall from a horse. The James, Younger, and Dalton brothers all chose the outlaw trail.

In 1830 Charles's son Henry wed Bursheba Fristoe. The marriage joined two of Missouri's leading families. Bursheba gave birth to fourteen babies—nine girls and five boys. Henry proved that he also had a knack for making money. His ferry business helped pay for land and slaves. One fine piece of land lay in the village of Strother. As the town grew it changed its name to Lee's Summit. Henry also found time to hold public office. One of "Judge" Younger's tasks was to help lay out county roads.

After three girls, Henry welcomed his first son in 1838. Dick was followed by two more girls. Cole arrived in 1844. The last three boys were Jim (b. 1848), John (b. 1851), and Bob (b. 1853).[1] The children grew up in a close and loving family. The boys spent long happy days hunting and fishing on Younger land. When Henry built a house, they worked beside him. As the girls came of age, Bursheba helped arrange their marriages. The local men thought the girls were good catches. It made sense to marry a woman whose father owned thousands of acres.

MINNESOTA
●Stillwater
●St. Paul
Northfield ●
Mankato ●

IOWA
●Adair
Corydon●

Liberty

ILLINOIS

Kansas
City
●Independence ●Alton
●Lee's Summit

Lawrence●

KANSAS

Harrisonville

Ste. Genevieve●
MISSOURI

●Russellville

KENTUCKY

Younger's Bend ●

OKLAHOMA

Scyene ●

TEXAS

THE YOUNGERS'
TERRITORY
1866—1875

● San Antonio

The deeds of the outlaw Younger brothers would one day be known from coast to coast, but their early years were spent on their father's farm in Lee's Summit, Missouri.

In 1859 the voters of Harrisonville picked Henry as their mayor. Mayor Younger and his sons ran the dry goods store and livery stable. His wagons carried mail across five hundred square miles. At home the Youngers put a high value on learning. Cole and Jim went to a school taught by Stephen Elkins. Elkins later went on to serve in the U.S. Senate. During the Civil War, Cole repaid any debt he owed his teacher. He saved Elkins's life when guerrillas wanted to kill him as a Yankee spy.

Dick emerged as the family star. At a time when few finished grade school, Henry's oldest boy earned a college degree. After he finished college, Dick came home to work beside his father. Henry hoped Cole would follow in his brother's footsteps, but the two boys were not alike. Where Dick was calm, Cole was ruled by impulse. Both were handsome, but Cole lacked his brother's polish. Only in strength and courage was Cole a match for Dick.

The rivalry ended one August night in 1860. Dick, only twenty-two, died of what may have been a burst appendix. All the siblings grieved, but the death changed Cole's life. College would have to wait. His duty, he believed, lay in helping his father. A man at sixteen, he did his best to take Dick's place.[2]

Whatever Cole's plans, events pushed them aside. Trouble was brewing along the Kansas-Missouri border. The dispute over slavery was about to drench the land with blood.

3

WAR COMES TO MISSOURI

———————————

Congress passed the Kansas-Nebraska Act in 1854. The act was meant to give settlers the right to vote for or against slavery. Instead, it brought war to western Missouri.

The conflict began when Missouri farmers staked out claims in Kansas. The claims gave them the vote— and they voted to make Kansas a slave state. Hot-headed Kansas "Free Staters" took up arms. Pro-slavers in Missouri formed their own bands of raiders. From 1855 on, the border region was torn by savage fighting.

The border conflict was part of a larger struggle. The South had long believed that its way of life depended on slave labor. In the North, antislavery feelings had grown stronger and stronger. Tensions increased in 1860 with the election of Abraham Lincoln. The South knew

13

the new President opposed slavery. Southern states began to leave the Union.

In April 1861 Southern guns fired on Fort Sumter, South Carolina. The attack plunged the nation into civil war. Fighting in the east spread to Missouri. Across the border the Free Staters grew bolder. That summer raiders stole horses and saddles from Henry Younger's livery stable. In September a larger force burned the town of Osceola.

Young Missourians formed their own guerrilla bands. The Jackson County boys were led by William Clark Quantrill. Cole was itching to join, but Henry held him back. Safety, the older man believed, lay in joining neither side.

A fight at a local dance tipped the scales. The trouble started when one of the Younger girls refused to dance with Irwin Walley. When the Union soldier persisted, Cole stepped between them. Walley turned on Cole and called him a Quantrill spy. Moments later the two men were wrestling on the floor. Fearing bloodshed, friends pulled them apart.

After he heard the story, Henry sent Cole into hiding. Walley, he guessed, would be back with an arrest warrant. Cole armed himself and took to the woods. Because it was wartime, that act made him an outlaw. In January 1862 he joined Quantrill for a daring raid on Hannibal, Missouri. Dressed as Union troops, the Southerners rode off with a large store of ammunition.

To stay neutral, Henry sold horses and supplies to both sides. Even so, the war caught up with him. On July 20, he spent the day in Kansas City. His business done, he headed home in his buggy. Friends found his body the next day, shot in the back. The Youngers blamed Irwin Walley.[1]

Cole and his friends swore revenge. They gunned down some soldiers said to have taken part in the murder. With the witnesses dead, a court released Walley for lack of proof. Cole claimed later that he pursued Walley, but never caught him. After the war, perhaps at Bursheba's request, he dropped his quest. "I could not pollute my soul with such a crime," he wrote.[2]

In August 1862 Cole tried a new trick. Dressed as an

William Clark Quantrill led a ruthless band of Missouri guerrillas during the Civil War. Cole and Jim Younger both rode with Quantrill. While he was with the raiders, Cole once dressed as a "granny" to spy on Union forces.

Quantrill's raiders sometimes attacked helpless settlers. In this engraving, a family flees from a burning farmhouse. At bottom right, two of the raiders ride off with their loot.

old woman, he rode into Independence, Missouri. As he sold his basket of apples, he took notes on the strength of the Union forces. The con game ended when an alert soldier grabbed "granny's" reins. Fearing capture, Cole whipped out a pistol and shot the man. Yankee bullets whizzed by him as he fled. Armed with Cole's report, Quantrill captured the town two days later.

Union troops found Bursheba at the family farm in early 1863. Ordered to reveal Cole's hideout, she refused. To punish her they burned the farmhouse. That summer Union troops threw the guerrillas' wives and sisters into a Kansas City prison.

Quantrill struck back by attacking Lawrence,

Kansas. The raid soon turned into a massacre. Outraged, the Union Army ordered the evacuation of three Missouri counties. Bursheba set her own house afire. The act, she said, denied Union troops the pleasure of burning it. Then she left to stay with her sister. A year later soldiers torched the sister's farm. John and Bob wanted to join the fight, but both were too young.

Cole joined the Confederate army. The new captain was sent to weed out Union supporters in Texas. By then sixteen-year-old Jim was riding with Quantrill. Even though the South gave up in April 1865, the guerrillas fought on. On May 10, soldiers trapped Quantrill in a barn and killed him. Jim was captured and sent to prison.[3]

In Missouri the end of the fighting brought little cheer. The wounds left by the war took a long time to heal.

4
DRIFTING INTO A
LIFE OF CRIME

The end of the war found Cole in California. With his army duty finished, he vacationed in San Jose with his uncle. Back in Missouri, Bursheba was pulling the family together. She returned to Strother and kept house for John, Bob, and two of her daughters. Jim rejoined her after he left prison. He gained his release by swearing loyalty to the Union.

Cole returned to spend Christmas at home. It was a risky visit. A court had charged him with an unsolved murder. A trial might have cleared him, but Cole went into hiding. With wartime passions still strong, he feared a trial would end in a lynching.[1] His fear may help explain why Cole joined forces with the James brothers. He was an outlaw in the eyes of the law. Why not rob a bank?

Except for young Wymore's death, the Liberty bank

job went like clockwork. The $15,000 in gold coins did cause a few headaches. Spending it close to home would draw too many questions. It was Cole's friend in Texas who solved the problem. If the outlaws met him in San Antonio, he would swap the gold for greenbacks. Jim said he would ride along with Cole, Frank, and Jesse.

The four men stopped in Scyene, Texas, on their way home. John Shirley, a Missouri native, opened his home to his old friends. What happened next is hard to pin down. Legend says that Shirley's teenage daughter fell in love with Cole. When she grew up, Myra Belle Shirley gained fame as Belle Starr, the Bandit Queen. Were Cole and Belle lovers? Two facts, at least, are certain. When Belle gave birth to a daughter she named the girl Pearl Younger. Also, in later years, Cole was a frequent guest at the ranch Belle called Younger's Bend.[2]

In October 1866 the James-Younger gang struck again. This time the boys stole $2,000 from a bank in Lexington, Missouri. As the news spread, the western states were hit by a wave of holdups. Most were blamed on the James-Younger gang. In fact, Cole was out of the state most of the year. He was thinking of starting a ranch near Scyene. Jesse was hiding out in Kentucky.

With lawmen looking for them in Missouri, the outlaws hit a bank in Kentucky. On March 20, 1868, Cole, Jesse, and Frank walked into Russellville's Long and Norton Bank. One of the outlaws asked Nimrod Long to cash a bond. In the next instant they drew their guns and jumped the counter. Long escaped through the back room as a bullet grazed his head. As firing broke out in the street, a clerk scooped $14,000 into the outlaws' sack. Then the outlaws bolted for their horses. Townsfolk blazed away as the horsemen fled, but their aim was poor. No one was hit.[3]

Rewards were posted, but the gang had plenty of friends. In the eyes of poor people, anyone who held up a bank was a hero. Many also sympathized with men who had risked their lives fighting for the South. Alarmed by their losses, the banks called in the Pinkerton National Detective Agency. A Pinkerton man soon learned the names of the Russellville bandits. Cole,

Belle Starr, who was later known as the "Bandit Queen," posed for this picture in 1887. When the Youngers first met her, she was a teenage girl living in Scyene, Texas. Tales of a love affair between Belle and Cole Younger cannot be proven.

Cole was riding with the James brothers when they robbed this bank in Russellville, Kentucky. The outlaws rode off with $14,000. In 1868, $14,000 was a huge sum of money.

Jesse, Frank, and the Shepard brothers topped the list. A posse managed to track down the Shepards. The lawmen shot Oliver. George was given a three-year sentence.[4]

With the law on his heels, Cole moved Bursheba to Scyene. Jim went into business with him there, buying and selling cattle. John and Bob stayed at the ranch to be near their mother, who was ill. Neither liked working with cattle, but family ties were strong.

In 1870 Cole and Jim served as census takers for Dallas County. On Sundays the family went to church. Jim and Bob sang in the choir. Bob fell in love with the preacher's daughter. For a time it seemed as though the family had found peace.

5

FOUR OUTLAW BROTHERS

In the spring of 1870 Bursheba knew that she was dying. Her last wish, she said, was to be buried near Henry.[1] Jim, with help from Bob and John, took their mother back to Missouri. Soon after their arrival, a posse rode up to the house. The men asked for Jim, but he was gone for the day.

The threat of arrest sent Jim hurrying back to Texas. The next time the posse appeared, the men asked for Cole, too. John refused to talk. To loosen his tongue, the men tied a rope around his neck. Then they hung him from a beam in the barn. When they yanked him up for the fourth time he passed out.

The shock of Jim's near-hanging was too much for Bursheba. She died a few days later. After the funeral the three boys returned to Texas. They tried to take up their old lives there, but failed. Bob's girlfriend broke off the engagement. John found work in Dallas, but still felt restless. When Jim proposed a trip to Missouri, all three joined him.

John returned to Scyene in January 1871—and found more trouble. He was hanging out in a saloon one night when a joke got out of hand. John took drunken aim and tried to shoot a pipe out of an old man's mouth. One bullet nicked the man's nose. The next day a deputy came to John's hotel to arrest him. Hard words and an escape attempt led to gunplay. When the smoke cleared the deputy lay dead. John limped away with shotgun pellets in his leg.[2]

The four Youngers met in Missouri that April. Cole invited Jim and John to join Jesse's gang. They turned him down. Jim drifted back to Texas. There he found a part-time job with the Dallas police. John said he would try his luck in California.

Cole had his heart set on sending Bob to college. Bob argued that he was poorly prepared for college work. Cole would not listen. He dropped Bob at the College of William and Mary in Virginia and went on to Florida. Bob did not stay long. He spent his college money for a trip through the South. Later he made up an excuse for Cole. The students, he lied, had shunned him because his brother was an outlaw.

By the spring of 1873 John was back in Missouri. He rode beside Cole when the gang robbed the bank in Ste. Genevieve. Bob was the next to join. He wanted to be

The James-Younger gang began robbing trains in 1873. In the first holdup the outlaws derailed the engine, killing the engineer. In later holdups, they lay in wait and took over the engine while it was stopped. Train crews knew better than to disobey orders shouted by trigger-happy gunslingers.

part of the train robbery Jesse and Frank were planning. As the daring plan matured, Jim returned and said he wanted in, too. For the first time the brothers would be riding the outlaw trail together.

In July, Cole and Jesse heard of a rich target. A train was scheduled to pass near Adair, Iowa, with $75,000 in its safe. When the engine hit the rails loosened by the gang, it jumped the tracks. The engineer died in the crash. Instead of $75,000, the gang found only $2,000 in the express car safe. The big money, it turned out, was on the next day's train.

The gang held up a second train at Gads Hill, Missouri, in January 1874. Afterward, Jim and John hid out at Monegaw Springs. Three Pinkerton men showed up in March, posing as cattle buyers. The Youngers saw through the disguise. They followed the detectives and ordered them to halt. One detective fled, but Louis Lull drew a hidden gun. His hurried shot caught John in the throat. As he fell, the dying outlaw killed Lull with a shotgun blast. Jim gunned down the third man. He buried John in an orchard before fleeing to California.[3]

That winter Cole and Bob helped steal $30,000 from a train at Muncie, Kansas. Bob used his share to lease a farm in Jackson County. With cash in his jeans, Cole spent some time in Kentucky. He must have laughed when he saw himself featured in a new book. *The Life, Character and Daring Exploits of the Younger Brothers* contained more fiction than fact.

6

THE $26 BANK ROBBERY

In mid-1876 Jesse James was looking for a fat and easy target. Bill Chadwell, a new gang member, assured him that the banks in Minnesota were bulging with cash. The farmers who lived there, Chadwell added, were "hayseeds."[1]

Jesse picked a small-town bank in Mankato. To add firepower he asked Bob Younger to join him. Bob was not an easy sell. The idea of working so far from home did not appeal to him. Jesse finally convinced him that Chadwell would make a good guide.

Cole took an instant dislike to the plan. He agreed to go only because Bob would not change his mind. He sent a wire to Jim, who had settled into a new life in California. "Come home," the wire said. "Bob needs you."[2] Reluctant but loyal, Jim rushed back to Missouri.

To finance the trip, the gang robbed a train at Rocky

Cut, Missouri. With $15,000 shared out, the eight men took a train to St. Paul in late August. They stayed in good hotels while they scouted the countryside. Some of their money went to buy horses and saddles. At night the outlaws drank and gambled the hours away.

On September 2, the gunmen met near Mankato. Bob and Jesse checked out the bank and brought back bad news. Construction work on the building had drawn a large crowd. Worse, Jesse thought he had been recognized. As spirits sagged, Chadwell offered a new plan.

Hanging out in saloons was a favorite pastime for the Youngers. In August 1876 they stopped off in St. Paul, Minnesota, to try their luck at the gambling tables. They might have stayed longer if they had known what lay ahead.

He said that the bank in Northfield was just as ripe for looting.[3]

The outlaws reached Northfield on September 7. The plan called for Bob, Jesse, and Frank to go into town for lunch. An hour later Cole and Clell Miller would station themselves near the bank. With their backup in place, the first three would enter the bank. Jim, Chadwell, and Charlie Pitts would be waiting on a nearby bridge. The sound of gunshots would bring them at the gallop, guns blazing.

At 2:00 P.M. Jesse led Bob and Frank into the First National Bank. Outside, Miller saw that the door was partly open. Before he could close it, a local merchant reached for the handle. Miller grabbed the man's arm, but it was too late. The merchant had seen too much. He jerked free and dashed around the corner. As he ran he shouted, "Get your guns, boys! They're robbing the bank!"[4]

Inside, the outlaws had their hands full. Cashier Joseph Heywood swore that the inner door of the vault was secured by a time lock. What he failed to say was that the time lock had been turned off. The door would have opened at a touch, but no one tried it. Bob grabbed what money he could find. When shooting started out in the street, teller A. E. Bunker dashed for the back door. Bob's snap shot hit him in the shoulder, but Bunker kept running.

Jim, Chadwell, and Pitts charged into the chaos of a

The luck of the James-Younger gang ran out at this Northfield, Minnesota bank (far left). Midway through the holdup, alert townsfolk opened fire. Rifle bullets killed two of the six gang members. Cole, Jim, and Bob escaped on horseback despite their wounds.

street battle. Medical student Henry Wheeler had opened fire from a second-story window. The first shot plugged Jim in the shoulder. Wheeler's next shot killed Miller. Cole waved his pistol and ordered bystander Nicolas Gustavson to go inside. The words were lost on the Swede, who did not speak English. A stray bullet killed him.

Cole rode up to the bank door. "They're killing our men! Get out here!" he yelled.[5] Store owner Anselm Manning put a bullet into Bob's waiting horse. Another bullet tore through Cole's thigh. A third killed Chadwell.

Bob and Jesse dashed out of the bank. Frank stayed behind long enough to kill Heywood. Wheeler's next shot hit Bob in the elbow. The James brothers mounted their horses and galloped toward open country. Cole reached down and pulled Bob onto his own horse. Moments later the last four gang members were raising dust on the trail out of Northfield.

The gunfight had lasted only eight minutes. Two outlaws and two townsmen lay dead or dying. All three Youngers were nursing painful wounds. The payoff was hardly worth the carnage. The gang rode off with a grand total of $26.70.[6]

Like his brother Jesse, Frank James learned the gunslinger's trade as one of Quantrill's raiders. After the war he became a charter member of the James-Younger gang. It was Frank who asked his friend Cole Younger to join the gang.

7
"WE'RE ALL DOWN EXCEPT ME"

The six surviving gang members met outside of town. In the distance they heard church bells calling Northfield to arms. Back in the town square a posse was forming. At the telegraph office the operator sent the news to towns near and far. A thousand riders took up the chase.[1]

The bloodstained outlaws stopped at the Cannon River to tend their wounds. All had been hit at least once. After stealing a horse for Bob, they rode ten miles to Shieldsville. Bob, weak from loss of blood, fell from his saddle. The quick-thinking Jesse pushed Bob back onto his horse.

Just then, four armed men stepped from a saloon. The outlaws drew their guns and shouted for the men to stay back. Then they galloped off and found shelter in the nearby woods. A posse saddled up and followed.

Catching sight of the outlaws in a ravine, the posse traded shots with the gang. This time it was rain that saved the fugitives. Hidden by a sudden downpour, the gang vanished into the dense undergrowth of the Big Woods.

Reports of gang sightings flooded in from all points. Posses crisscrossed the state. A bluff carried the outlaws past one checkpoint. We're part of a posse, they claimed. Near Janesville the fugitives stole four fresh horses. A posse nearly trapped them, but they vanished again in the thick woods.

The gang covered only six miles in two days. After spotting a large posse near Lake Elysian, the fugitives hid on an island. With the lawmen closing in they left their horses behind. The trick worked because the patrols were watching for men on horseback. Safe for the moment, progress was slower than ever. Bob was running a fever. Jim's wound was bleeding. Cole limped along with the aid of a stout stick.

About ten miles from Mankato, the outlaws holed up at a deserted farm. The rest was welcome, but food was scarce. On September 12, they stole more horses. Soaked by the rain, horses and riders slogged through deep mud.

On September 14, Bob offered to stay behind. Without him, he said, the rest would have a better chance. Cole and Jim refused, but Jesse sided with Bob. He argued that they all would have a better chance if they

Three of the outlaw Younger brothers—Bob (left), Jim (center), and Cole (right)—were photographed soon after their capture in September, 1876. The bandage on Jim's upper lip marks the broken jaw he suffered in the final shootout. Jim and Cole survived their years behind bars, but Bob died in prison.

split up. The Youngers agreed. They sent the Jameses off with the last two horses. Riding fast and hard, Jesse and Frank found safety in South Dakota.

A week later farmboy Oscar Sorbel spotted Cole, Bob, Jim, and Pitts. He rode to town and reported to Sheriff James Glispin. The lawman tracked the gang to a boggy spot called Hanska Slough. Wary of the Youngers' marksmanship, his posse opened fire at long range. The fugitives scrambled for cover.

Seven brave lawmen inched closer to the outlaws' willow thicket. One of them put a bullet through Pitts's heart. Another slug smashed Jim's jaw. A third plowed into Cole's head. Bob waved a white rag and yelled,

"Hold your fire! We're all down except me."[2] As he stumbled forward, a final shot rang out. He fell backward, blood streaming from his chest.[3]

The lawmen loaded their captives into a wagon. At Madelia the townsfolk gathered to stare at the famed outlaws. Despite his eleven wounds, Cole was game to the last. Hearing the cheers, he stood and tipped his hat to the crowd. From Madelia the wagon carried the prisoners to Faribault. There a doctor dressed their wounds.

Two months later the Youngers went on trial. They did not expect mercy. As Bob told a reporter, "We are rough men and used to rough ways."[4] Each entered a guilty plea to charges of murder and robbery. The guilty pleas saved their lives. Instead of a hangman's noose, each drew a life sentence.

8

A LONG WAIT FOR PAROLE

———————◆▸◆◂◆———————

The iron gates of Minnesota's Stillwater Prison clanged behind the Youngers in November 1876. Ahead lay endless days of what convicts call "hard time." Cole, Jim, and Bob wore the black-and-white stripes of third-grade prisoners. Luxuries were few. Each was confined to a tiny 5 x 7-foot cell. The cells contained a bed, water jar, mirror, and the Bible. During the day the brothers made buckets in a basement workshop.

The Youngers surprised the guards who thought they would be troublemakers. Good conduct earned them extra privileges. As second-grade prisoners they exchanged their stripes for gray-and-black checked outfits. They could let their hair grow and write two letters a month. Visits from family members were limited to one a month. As before, daily contact with each other was forbidden. The brothers were allowed to meet only once a month.

Second-grade prisoners also stepped up to better jobs. Bob painted walls until his injured elbow forced him to quit. After that he worked with Cole and Jim, making parts for farm machines. In their free time all three turned to books. Cole liked to read about the lives of great men and women. Jim favored religious works. Medicine was Bob's passion; he chose medical texts and magazines.[1]

All three Youngers lived with constant pain. Jim's shattered jawbone forced him to take his meals through a straw. A bullet lodged close to his brain caused severe headaches. He grew more and more depressed. Along with his bad elbow, Bob suffered from colds and fevers. His damp cell made the colds worse. Like Jim, Cole was often wracked by blinding headaches.

In 1882 news of Jesse's murder reached the prison. Bob was upset, but Cole and Jim felt only relief. No longer would the public fear a rebirth of the James-Younger gang. Because they were model prisoners, the warden picked the Youngers to be trusties. Their new status meant more freedom and better jobs. Cole worked in the hospital. Jim took charge of the prison mail. Later he worked in the library and helped start a prison newspaper. To fill the empty hours Cole and Jim took up woodworking. Bob kept mostly to himself. His cough had become chronic.

Fire broke out in 1884. Guards turned to the Youngers for help. They handed Cole a pistol and told him to watch the other convicts. Jim and Bob backed Cole with an ax and an iron bar. With their usual coolness, the three led the women inmates to safety. When the danger was past, they gave up their weapons. Reporters were amazed to learn they had not tried to escape.[2]

The Youngers came up for parole in 1886. Dreams of an early release had helped them survive the first ten years. Thomas Crittenden, an ex-governor of Missouri, spoke out in their defense. Friends and relatives raised money to speed their release. In Minnesota, however, memories of the Northfield raid had not faded. State

The Younger family never gave up hope that Cole, Jim, and Bob would be paroled. In 1889, Retta (standing, center) visited her brothers at the Stillwater, Minnesota prison. She posed for this photo with Bob (left), Cole (right), and Jim (seated, center). Bob was suffering from the illness that would kill him at age thirty-five.

Jim Younger tried to start a new life after he was paroled in 1901. Haunted by his past, he was not allowed to marry or hold a job that involved trust. Depressed and lonely, Jim took his own life in 1902.

officials felt the pressure. Months and years rolled past. The Youngers remained in prison.

Bob's health failed. In 1889 prison doctors found that he had tuberculosis. News that he was dying led to new calls for parole. The governor heard the pleas, but refused to sign a pardon. Over and over Bob asked his brothers to forgive him. He still felt guilty for dragging them into the mess in Minnesota. Cole tried to ease his brother's conscience, but could not. On September 16, 1889, Bob Younger died in his hospital bed.

The years slipped by. In 1901 a new state law gave Cole and Jim fresh hope. The law offered lifers a parole after twenty-four years. The last two Younger brothers had already served twenty-five years.

9

THE LEGEND GROWS

Cole was fifty-seven when he won his parole. Jim was fifty-three. The brothers had to promise not to leave Minnesota. They also agreed to take jobs approved by the state. As the day of their release neared, offers flooded in. The parole board sent them to a firm that made tombstones. When he left prison Jim went to work in the office. Cole traveled the county by buggy, drumming up sales. Each earned $60 a month.

Jim kept to himself. On most nights he was in bed by 8:00 P.M. After he hurt his back in a buggy accident he left the tombstone company. His next job was as a clerk in a cigar store. Illness cost him that job, and a failing business cost him another. Because he was in love, he kept trying. Alice Miller, a reporter he met while in prison, agreed to marry him. Their plans floundered because ex-cons could not sign contracts—not even a marriage contract. Alice moved out of state and Jim turned to selling insurance. He soon ran into the same roadblock. Depressed and ill, he told a friend, "I'm a ghost, the ghost of Jim Younger."[1] Two days later he shot himself.

Cole enjoyed his new life as much as Jim felt burdened by his. For pleasure he took in plays and went to dances. He was a regular churchgoer. His joints ached, but he stayed cheerful. Like Jim, he tried a number of jobs. Some of his best friends were policemen.

The long-sought pardon came through in February 1903. Free at last, Cole returned home to Missouri. Secure with family and friends, he worked on his memoirs. Among his visitors was Frank James.

Set free by a friendly jury, Frank James gave up the outlaw life. When Cole Younger returned to Missouri in 1903, Frank dropped by to renew their friendship. After Frank's death in 1915, Cole was the sole surviving member of the gang.

From 1909 to 1912, Cole worked the lecture circuit. At each stop he talked about the lessons he had learned in his life. When his health began to fail, he retired to Lee's Summit, Missouri. The last of the outlaw Younger brothers died there in 1916.

Although it broke the terms of his pardon, Cole joined Frank in a wild west show. Eager fans crowded close to ask for the famous outlaws' autographs.[2]

In 1909 Cole toured the Midwest as a lecturer. He called his talk, "What Life Has Taught Me." At each stop he urged young people to avoid the pitfalls that lead to crime.[3] After three years on the lecture circuit he retired. His niece, Nora Hall, kept house for him in Lee's Summit. Cole often sat on the front porch, chatting with visitors. He never talked about his outlaw days.

Cole always claimed that he carried eleven bullets in his body. In the end it was his heart and kidneys that failed. By the fall of 1915 he could no longer leave his bedroom. Cole died on March 21, 1916, with his family standing by. He was seventy-two years old.

Death did not close the books on the Youngers. As with other famous outlaws, their exploits grew to be larger than life. Tales that the James-Younger gang left buried money behind still lure treasure hunters. In truth, the gang robbed only a dozen banks and seven trains. The loot was soon spent.[4]

Stories that paint the Youngers as vicious killers are overblown. One Civil War tale has Cole "testing" a new rifle on captured Yankees. Cole hotly denied the story. On the other hand, the Youngers were quick on the trigger. As boys they had witnessed the bloody border wars. Cole and Jim came to manhood during the Civil War. Those hard times produced hard men.

Today the Youngers live on in books and films. Did they live the thrilling life we see on the screen? To those who see glamour in the outlaw life, Cole has a ready answer. "No mention is made of the hunted, hounded existence," he told a reporter. "No mention is made of . . . a violent death or a prison cell."[5] Straight talk was always a Younger trademark.

NOTES BY CHAPTER

Chapter 1
1. Carl Breihan, *The Day Jesse James Was Killed* (New York: Frederick Fell, 1961), p. 46.

2. Bill O'Neal, *Encyclopedia of Western Gunfighters* (Norman, Okla.: University of Oklahoma Press, 1979), p. 346.

3. James D. Horan, *The Authentic Wild West: The Outlaws* (New York: Crown Publishers, 1977), p. 37.

4. Quoted in Marley Brant, *The Outlaw Youngers: A Confederate Brotherhood* (Lanham, Md.: Madison Books, 1992), p. 76.

Chapter 2
1. Stewart Sifakis, *Who Was Who in the Civil War* (New York: Facts on File, 1988), p. 738.

2. Marley Brant, *The Outlaw Youngers: A Confederate Brotherhood* (Lanham, Md.: Madison Books, 1992), pp. 14–15.

Chapter 3
1. Marley Brant, *The Outlaw Youngers: A Confederate Brotherhood* (Lanham, Md.: Madison Books, 1992), p. 31.

2. Letter from Cole Younger to J. W. Buel, October 31, 1880.

3. Jay R. Nash, *Encyclopedia of World Crime* (Wilmette, Ill.: Crime Books, 1990), p. 3212.

Chapter 4
1. Howard Lamar, ed., *The Reader's Encyclopedia of the American West* (New York: Thomas Crowell, 1977), p. 1302.

2. Harry Sinclair Drago, *Road Agents and Train Robbers* (New York: Dodd, Mead and Co., 1973), pp. 155–156.

3. Harry Sinclair Drago, *Outlaws on Horseback* (New York: Bramhall House, 1964), p. 44.

4. Marley Brant, *The Outlaw Youngers: A Confederate Brotherhood* (Lanham, Md.: Madison Books, 1992), pp. 85–86.

Chapter 5
1. Marley Brant, *The Outlaw Youngers: A Confederate Brotherhood* (Lanham, Md.: Madison Books, 1992), p. 93.

2. Harry Sinclair Drago, *Outlaws on Horseback* (New York: Bramhall House, 1964), pp. 49–50.

3. Paul Trachtman and the Editors of Time-Life Books, *The Gunfighters* (Alexandria, Va.: Time-Life Books, 1974), p. 68.

Chapter 6

1. Harry Sinclair Drago, *Outlaws on Horseback* (New York: Bramhall House, 1964), p. 65.

2. Marley Brant, *The Outlaw Youngers: A Confederate Brotherhood* (Lanham, Md.: Madison Books, 1992), p. 164.

3. Drago, *Outlaws on Horseback*, p. 69.

4. James D. Horan, *The Authentic Wild West: The Outlaws* (New York: Crown Publishers, 1977), p. 67.

5. Ibid. p. 71.

6. Brant, p. 183.

Chapter 7

1. Harry Sinclair Drago, *Outlaws on Horseback* (New York: Bramhall House, 1964), p. 74.

2. Ibid. p. 76.

3. Bill O'Neal, *Encyclopedia of Western Gunfighters* (Norman, Okla.: University of Oklahoma Press, 1979), p. 347.

4. Ibid. p. 345.

Chapter 8

1. Marley Brant, *The Outlaw Youngers: A Confederate Brotherhood* (Lanham, Md.: Madison Books, 1992), pp. 216–218.

2. Ibid. p. 227.

Chapter 9

1. Quoted in Marley Brant, *The Outlaw Youngers: A Confederate Brotherhood* (Lanham, Md.: Madison Books, 1992), p. 280.

2. James D. Horan, *The Authentic Wild West: The Outlaws* (New York: Crown Publishers, 1977), p. 141.

3. Paul Trachtman and the Editors of Time-Life Books, *The Gunfighters* (Alexandria, Va.: Time-Life Books, 1974), p. 86.

4. Harry Sinclair Drago, *Outlaws on Horseback* (New York: Bramhall House, 1964), p. 40.

5. Quoted in Brant, p. 308.

GLOSSARY

bonds—A certificate of debt that guarantees payment of interest and principle, issued by a corporation or a governmental body.

census taker—Someone hired by the government to count the number of people living in a particular area.

contracts—Legal, binding agreements signed by two or more parties.

cuss—Western slang for "curse," as in "cuss word" or "that stubborn old cuss."

deputy—A lawman who assists a sheriff or marshal.

dime novels—Low-cost magazines that printed popular fiction during the late 1800s.

evacuation—The forced removal of an entire population.

express car—A special baggage car equipped to carry a train's cargo of mail, gold, cash, and other valuables.

Free Staters—Residents of Kansas during the 1850s who believed that their territory should reject slavery.

greenbacks—A slang term for U.S. paper money.

guerrillas—A small, fast-moving force of raiders who operate outside the normal laws of warfare.

legend—A story that many people believe, but which is often untrue in whole or in part.

livery stable—A business that houses, rents, and sells horses and wagons.

loyalty oath—A sworn promise to support the United States Constitution and to obey the laws that govern the nation.

lynching—The hanging of an accused criminal by an out-of-control mob.

massacre—The senseless killing of large numbers of people.

memoirs—Autobiographical accounts of a person's life.

pardon—A document that forgives an accused person of any crimes he or she may have committed. Most pardons for criminal acts are issued by state governors.

parole—The conditional release of a prisoner from jail before his or her sentence has been completed.

posse—A group of citizens who join with lawmen to help capture fleeing outlaws.

trusties—Prisoners who have earned special privileges by their good behavior.

tuberculosis—A contagious disease that attacks and destroys the lining of the lungs.

vault—The steel-walled strongroom where a bank stores money, bonds, and other valuables.

MORE GOOD READING ABOUT THE YOUNGER BROTHERS

Appler, Augustus C. *The Life, Character and Daring Exploits of the Younger Brothers.* St. Louis: Eureka Publishing Co., 1876.

Brant, Marley. *The Outlaw Youngers: A Confederate Brotherhood.* Lanham, Md.: Madison Books, 1992.

Breihan, Carl W. *The Complete and Authentic Life of Jesse James.* New York: Frederick Fell, 1953.

Drago, Harry Sinclair. *Outlaws on Horseback.* New York: Bramhall House, 1964, pp. 1–89.

Horan, James D. *The Authentic Wild West: The Outlaws.* New York: Crown Publishers, 1977, pp. 29–146.

Shirley, Glenn. *Belle Starr and Her Times.* Norman, Okla.: University of Oklahoma Press, 1982, pp. 63–96.

Sutton, William A., Jr. *Jesse James Was His Name.* Columbia, Mo.: University of Missouri Press, 1966.

Trachtman, Paul, and the Editors of Time-Life Books. *The Gunfighters.* Alexandria, Va.: Time-Life Books, 1974, pp. 52–87.

Younger, Cole. *Cole Younger By Himself.* Chicago: The Henneberry Co., 1903.

INDEX